How to Find Shark Teeth

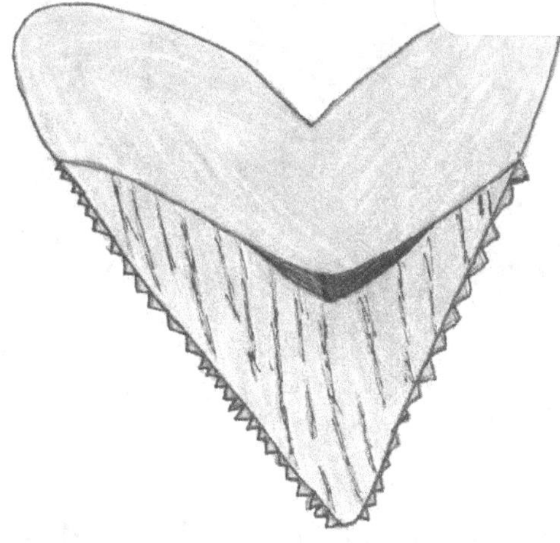

Adrian DeMarco

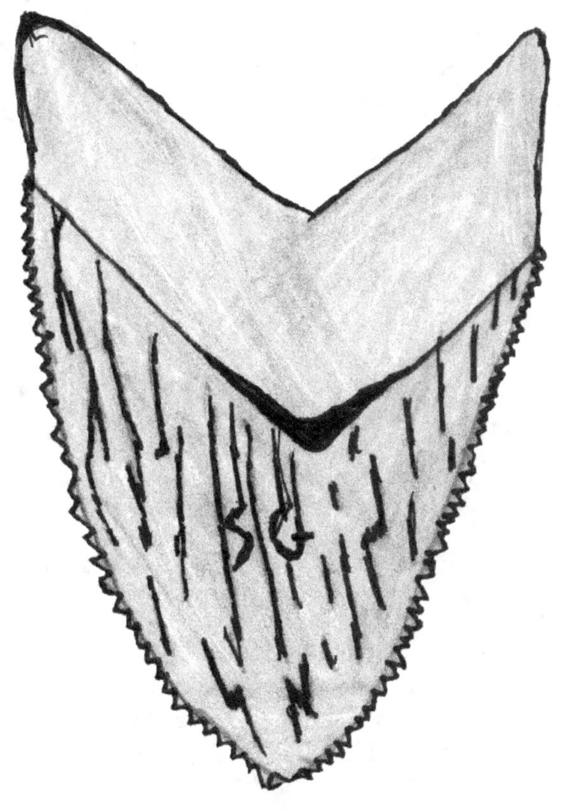

Fossil Hunter

venice Florida beach

things you need
★ sandfleacrake

First walk in the water with the sand flea rake and scoop some shells. Then sift the shells and look for shark teeth.

venice florida
beach
⭐ sifter
⭐ shovel
First go in the water
and take a scoop,
Then put the
scoop in the
sifter and
sift it and
find shark
teeth

3

Juno

☆ bag

First find shelly gravel near the water. Then wake the beach and look if you find one and put it in your bag and if you find a red and white and it is an seaurchin spike.

peace river

★ sifter

★ shovel

first go take a
scoop and put
it in the sifter
and sift it
and find fossils and
shark teeth

Horse
tooth

crocodile
tooth

little guide

mamith
tooth

alligator
tooth

sting
ray
mouth
plate

shark
tooth

puffer
fish
tooth

sting
ray
tail
part

5

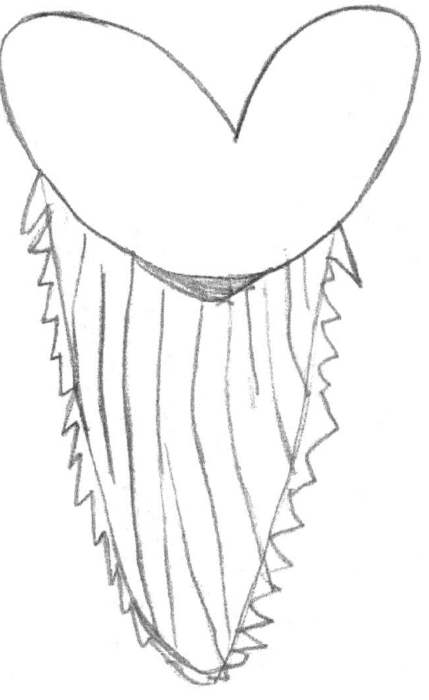

guide

pufferfish
tooth

Bull
—2 in
—2 in

mako
—1 in
—2 in
—3 in

great white
—1 in
—2 in
—3 in
—4 in

lemon
—1 in
—2 in

sting
ray
in1
in2
in3
in4
in5

sand
tiger
in 1
in2
in3

sting
ray
mouth
plate
in1
in2

tiger

part meg
ancestor
in1
in2
in3
in4
in5
in6
in7

megalodon

☆ bag
☆ water shoes
☆ sun block
☆ water

☆ sifter
☆ shovel

☆ sand flea rake
☆ nat geo scooper

8

venice florida
beach map
south
venice

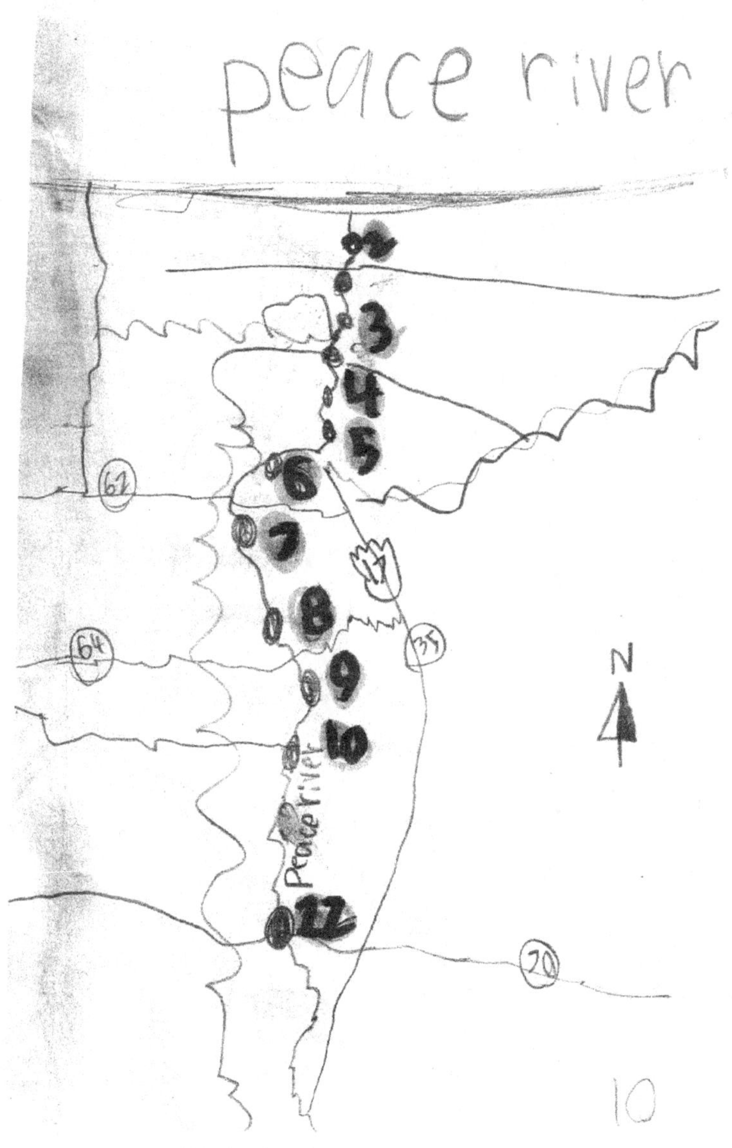

10

Juho
708
1
tequesta
jupiter
95
706
95
10
Juno
Pier
Juno
beach
pallm
Gardens beach
North
Palm
beach
Riviera
beach
704A

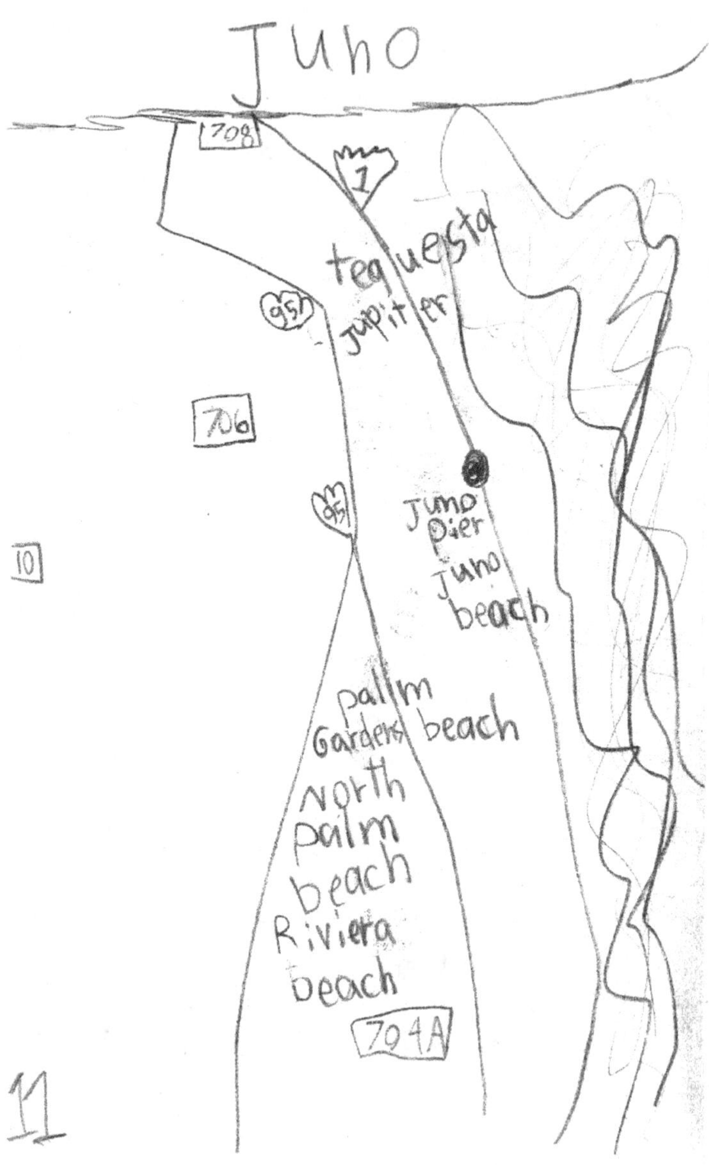

11

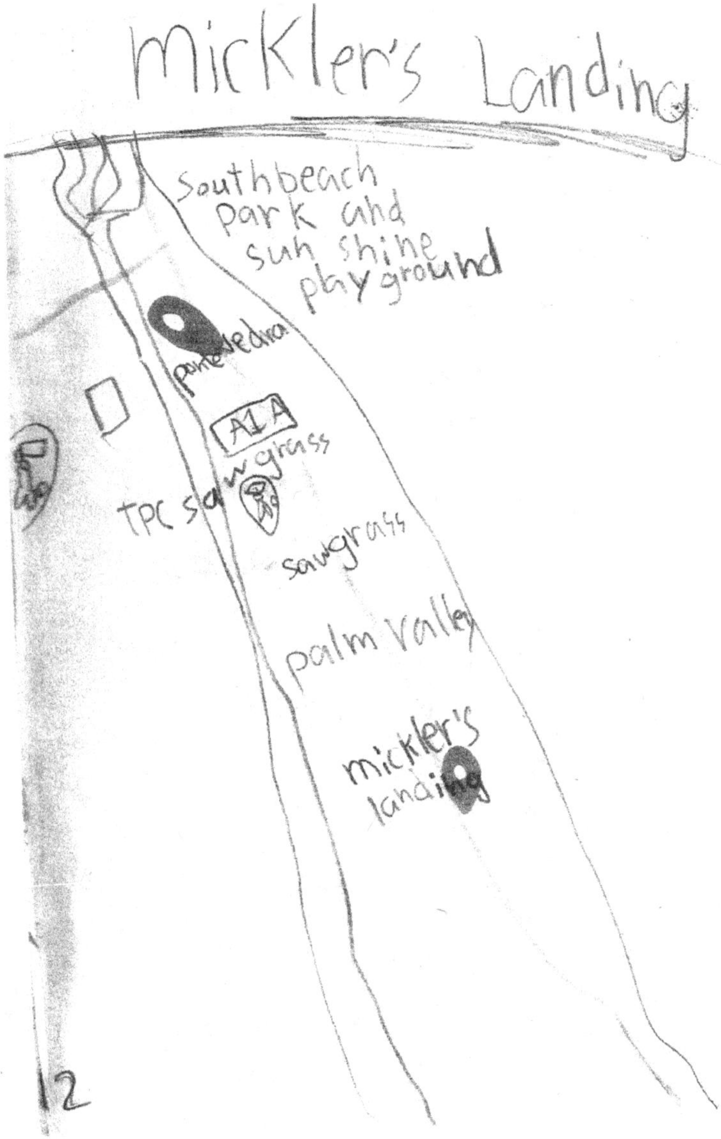
mickler's Landing
southbeach park and sun shine playground
ponte vedra
A1A
TPC sawgrass
sawgrass
palm valley
mickler's landing

mickler's Landing

first find
a gravelly
area where
the water
touches
then start
looking
and find
shark teeth

for rivers
and
Venice

NO! collecting
arrowhead
NO! if you have a
you cut and
are and
NO! red tide in
Do
no stealing Not
shark teeth go
only if in
the person the
tells you. Water.

14

Bonus Material

bone   valley

★ hose

★ shovel

★ sifter

★ water shoes

first shoel some mud and put the scoop in the sifeter and spray on the sifter and find shark teeth.

ahsester megladon

secret place

road side
in venice

red tide
alligator's
cut's

things
Needed

water shoes

water

sun block

patlbord

food

sifter

Shovel

sand flea rake

Venice

★ sand flearake
★ shovel
★ sifter

First go wast deep a scoop with the shovelor sand flearake and put it in the sifter and sift it and find shark teeth.

Diveing
First go 30 feet Down and find gravel and shark teeth.

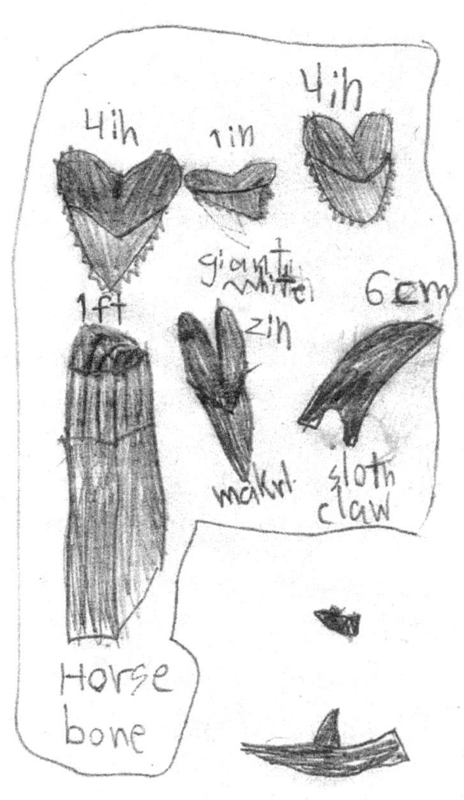

4ih
1in
4ih
giant white
zin
6 cm
1ft
makrl
sloth claw
Horse bone

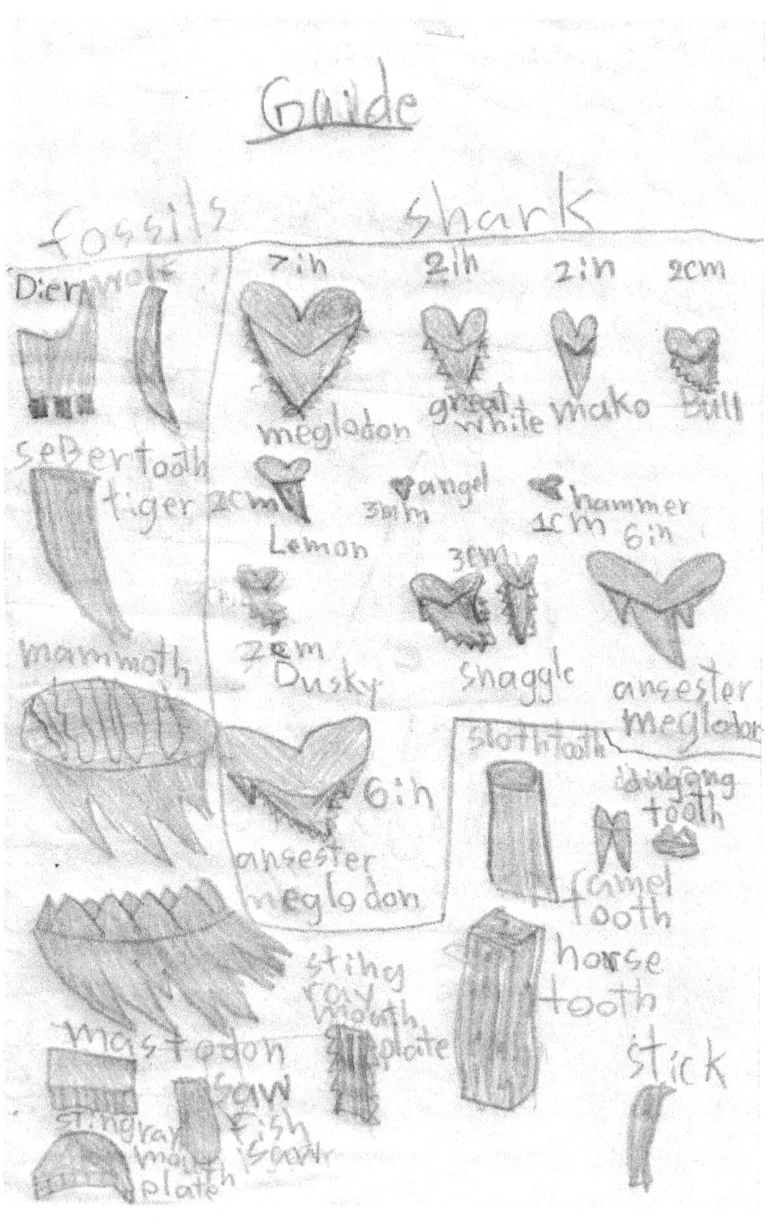
Guide
fossils
shark
Dierwolf
7in
2in
2in
2cm
megladon
great white
mako
Bull
seBertooth tiger
2cm
angel
3in
hammer
1cm
6in
Lemon
mammoth
3cm
2cm
Dusky
Snaggle
ansester meglodon
6in
slothtooth
dugong tooth
ansester meglodon
camel tooth
horse tooth
sting ray mouth plate
mastodon
stick
saw fish saw
stingray mouth plate

24

How to find
shark teeth

More Books coming soon
How to find mollusk fossils
How to find shark teeth
fossil farm
How to find shark teeth
How to find shark teeth for experts
winner
How to find shark teeth

How to Find Shark Teeth